It was Kipper's birthday.

Kipper wanted a party.

Everyone wanted to come.

Biff put up balloons.

4

Mum made a cake.

Dad took a sandwich.

'Stop it,' said Mum.

Everyone came to the party.

Dad wanted to play a game.

But Kipper put the television on.

'Oh no!' said Mum, 'What a mess!'

The children played with the bubbles.

'What a good party!' everyone said.